C

Think - What part ody do you know?
Guess - Are the names of animal body parts the same as humans?

1. Human bodies

Humans and animals have bodies. Each part of the body has a name.

Body

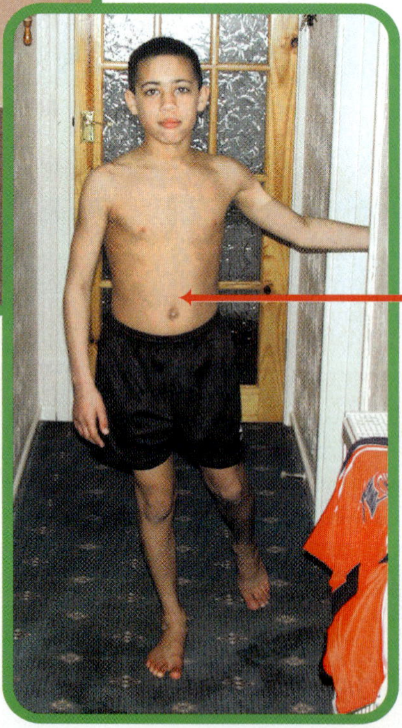

Body

Animal bodies

Sometimes the name is the same for both humans and animals, sometimes it is different.

Bodies
Heads
Chests
Legs
Arms

2. Human heads

The head is the most important part of our body. Inside our head is our brain. It is the brain that tells the rest of the body to think, see and talk.

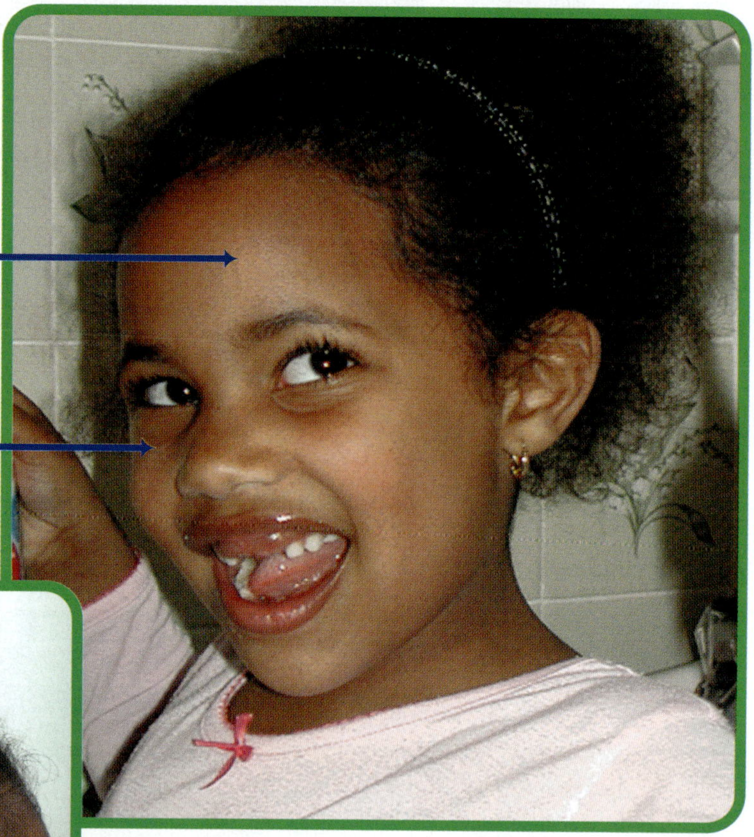

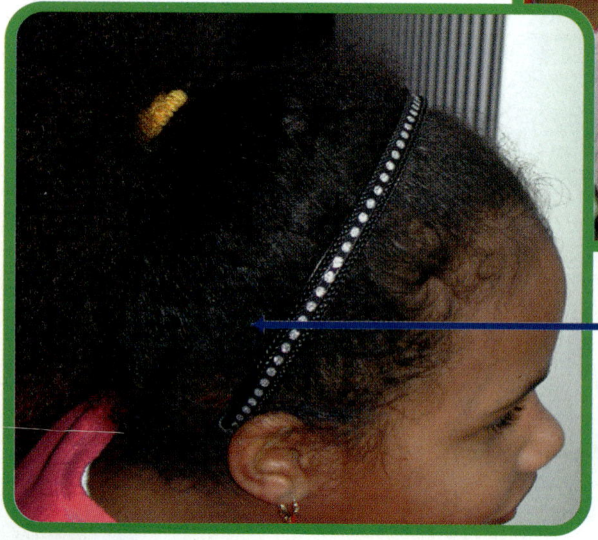

Animal heads

Head

Head

All animals have heads. But the brains of animals are much smaller than human brains. Animals have eyes, noses and mouths but they are all very different to humans.

Head

Head

3. Human chests

The chest is the biggest part of our body. Inside the chest are our important organs. Our heart and lungs are in our chests.

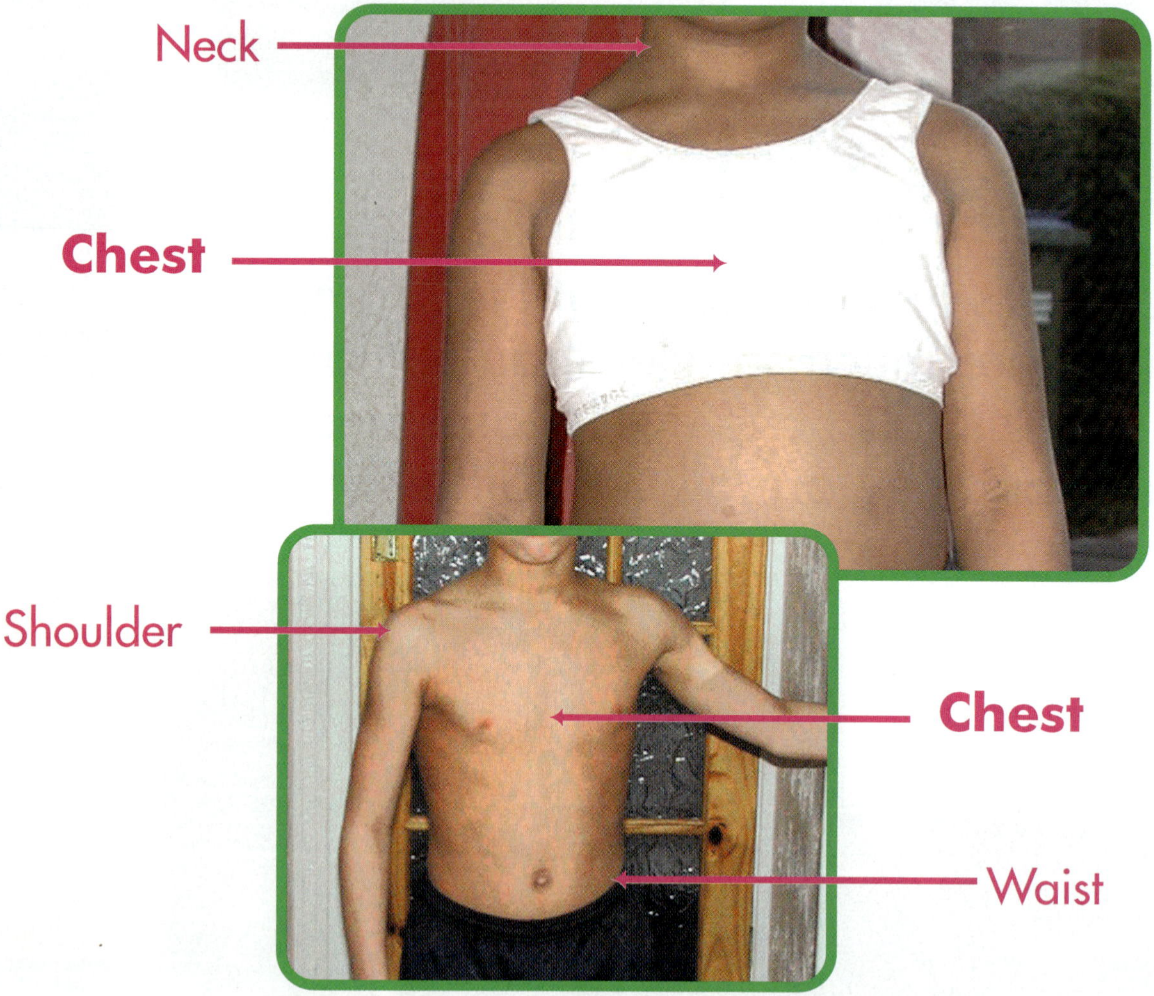

Animal chests

Chest

Breast

Each animal has a part of the body that has important organs in it.

Chest

Thorax

4. Human legs

Humans (and birds) only have two legs. Knees allow us to bend our legs. Ankles allow us to move our feet.

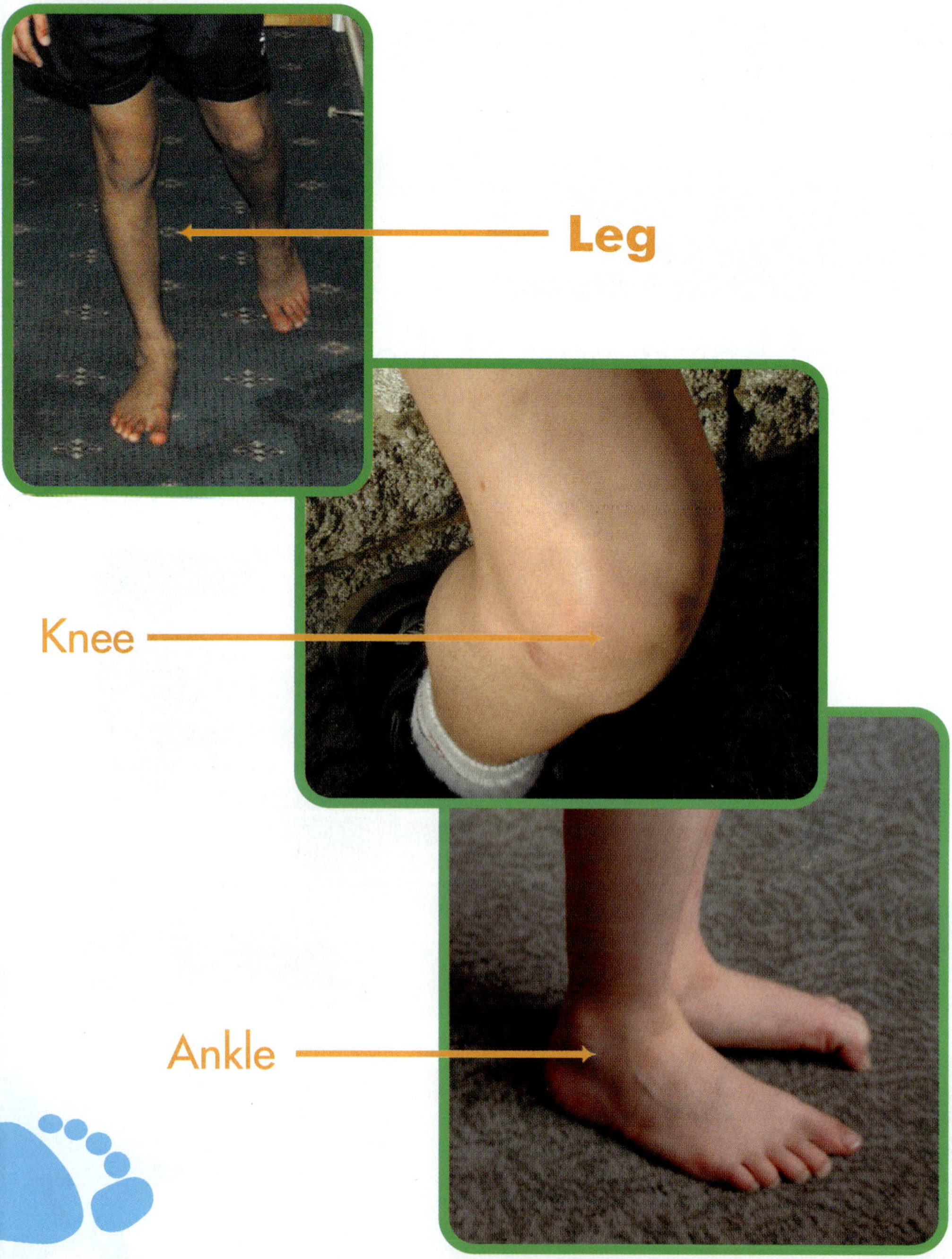

Animal legs

Legs are very important to most animals but they differ in their length, width, shape and number.

5. Arms

Humans (and only a few animals) have arms. They are very useful to us because we can move them in lots of different ways.

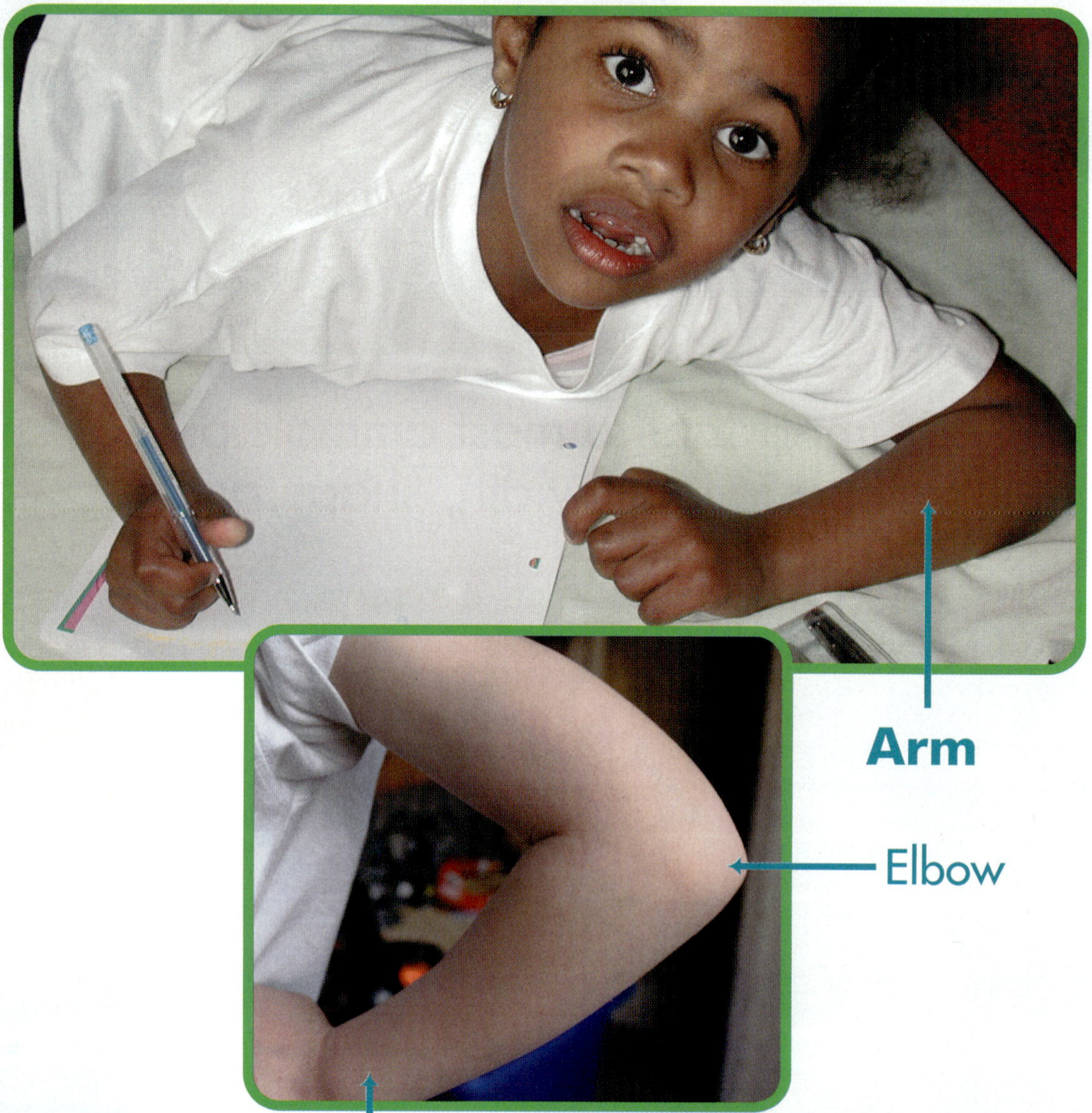

Arms

The animals in this book cannot do these things because they do not have arms.

Throwing

Catching

Holding

Writing

6. Human hands and feet

Human's hands have many moving parts.

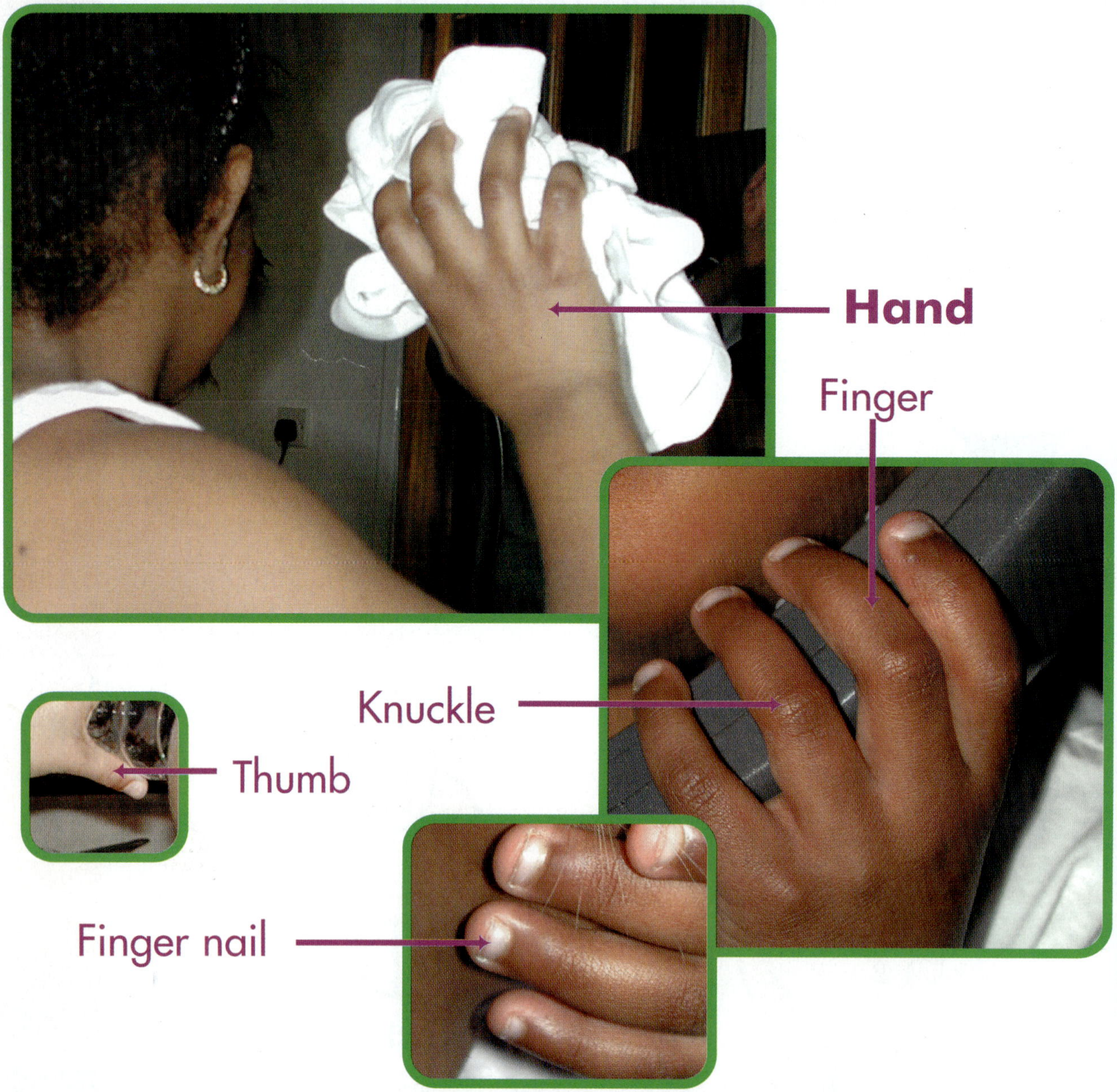

Hands allow us to do many things

Human hands and feet

Feet are useful to us.

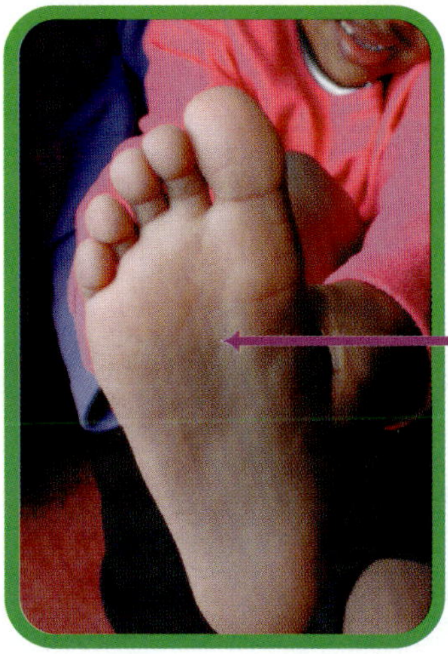

Sole

Ankle

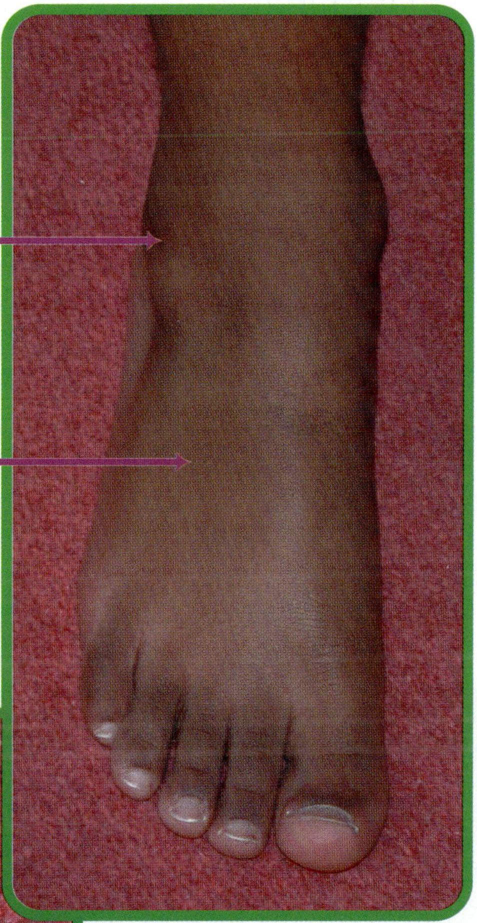

Foot

Toe

Toe nail

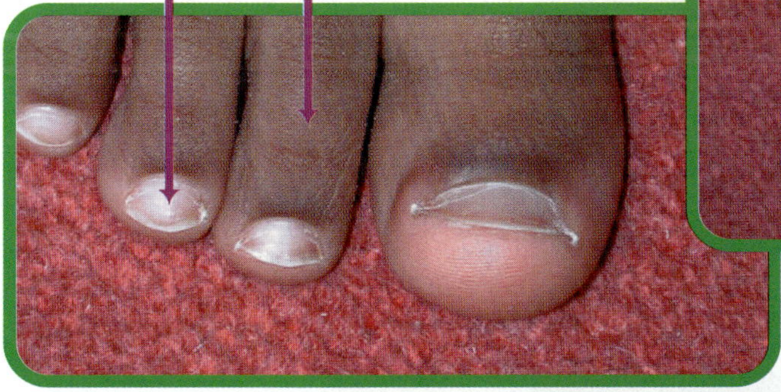

Our feet allow us to do many things but we use them in a different way to our hands.

Human hands and feet
Animal feet
Backs
Faces
Animal parts

7. Animal feet

All animals have feet. They differ in their shape and size. Each kind of animal has feet that are right for the place it lives and how it moves.

Feet for flying and resting on plants

Feet for dry hot ground

Animal feet

Feet for climbing and swimming

Feet for swimming and walking

Human hands and feet
Animal feet
Backs
Faces
Animal parts

8. Backs

Humans have backbones. Our backbone is a number of small bones in a long line.

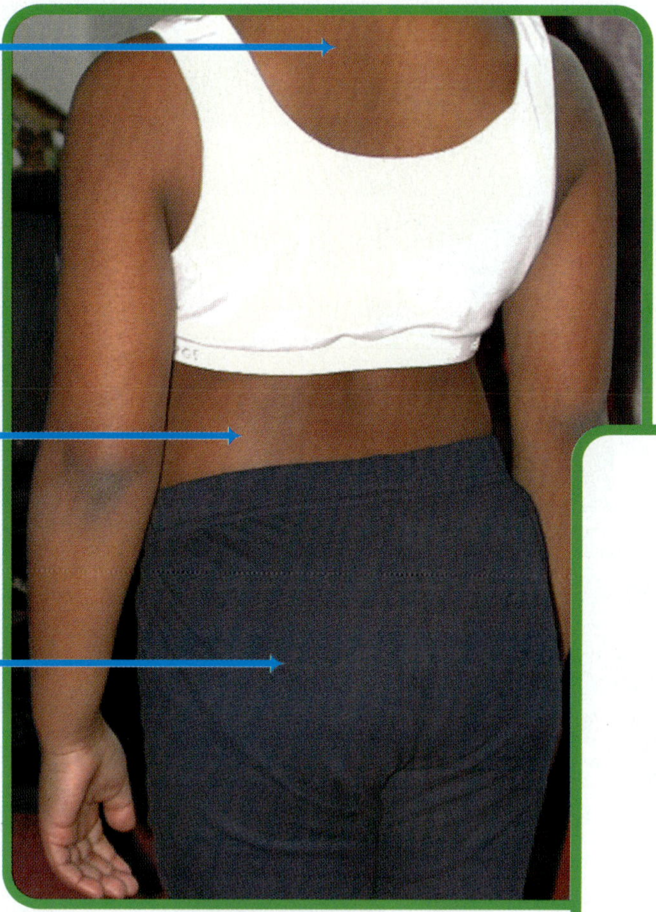

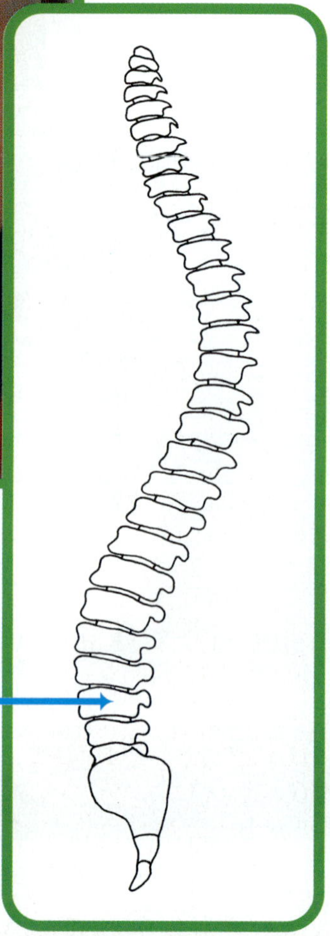

Backs

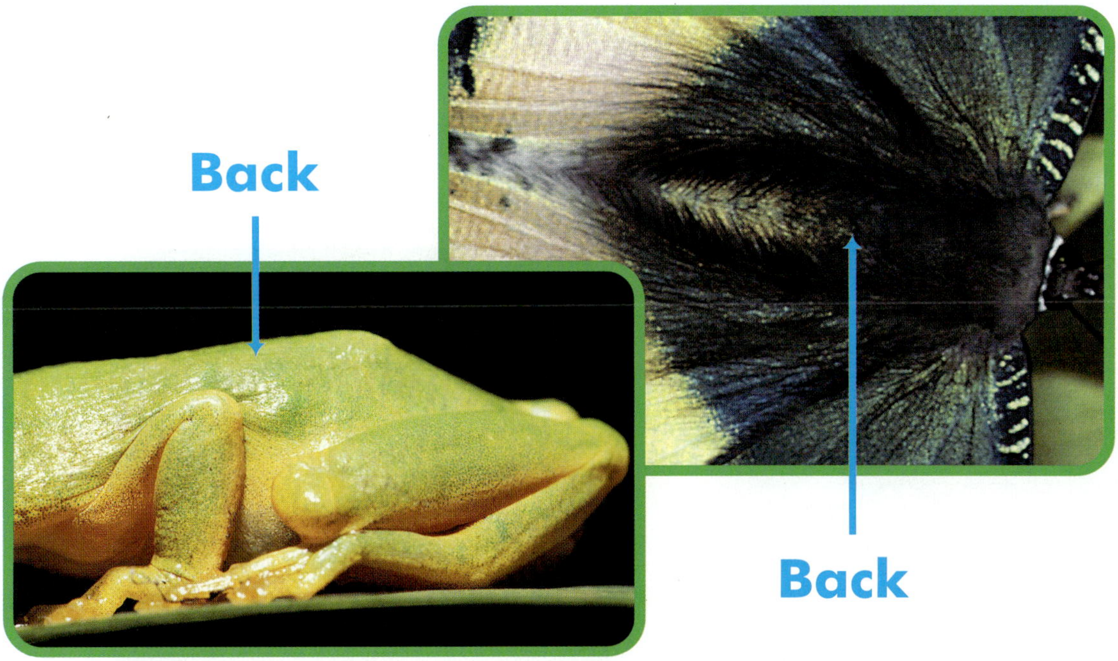

Some of the smaller animals do not have backbones.

9. Human faces

Every human face is different, but each one has the same body parts.

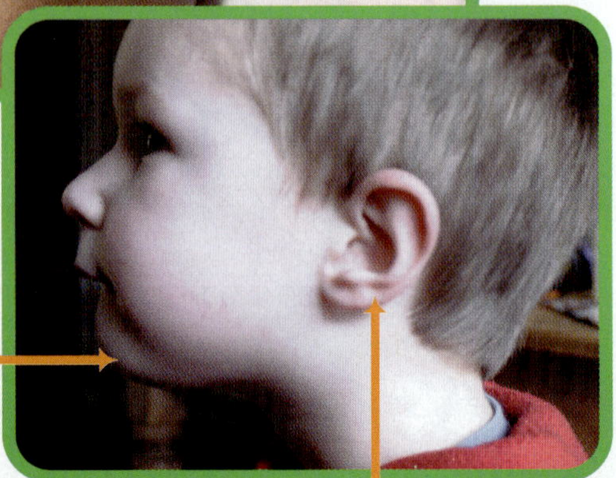

Human faces

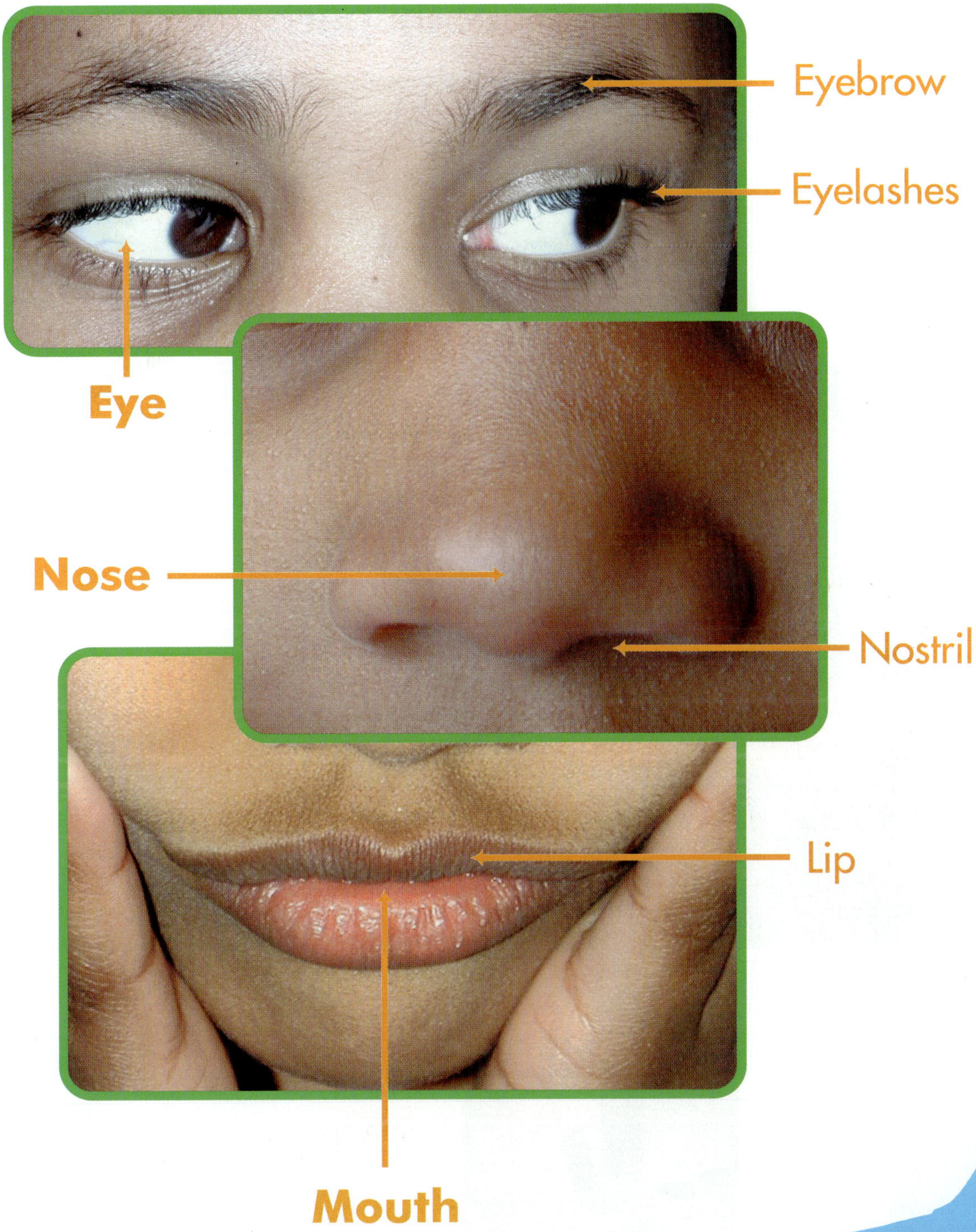

11. Animal body parts

Humans do not have these body parts.

Animal body parts

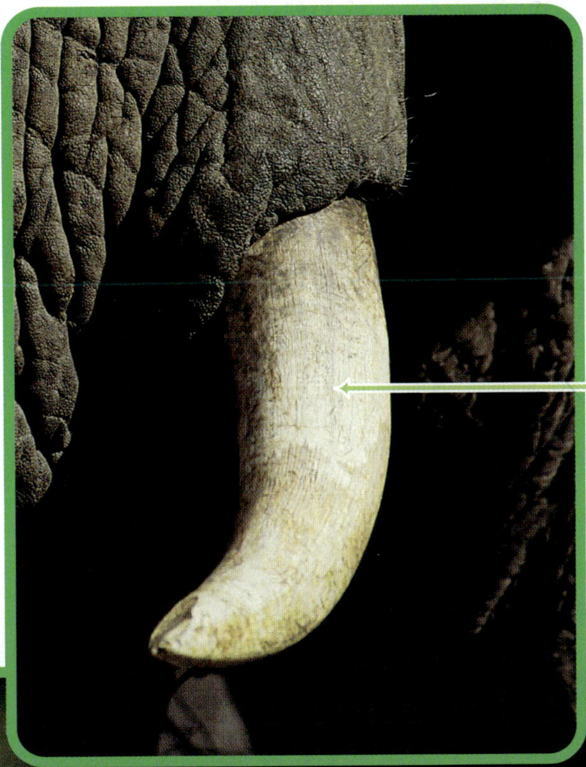

Human hands and feet
Animal feet
Backs
Faces
Animal parts

Activity page

Head

Leg

Thumb

Elbow

Foot

Knee

Feet

Head

Thorax

Legs

Trunk

Antennae

Breast

Eye

Mouth

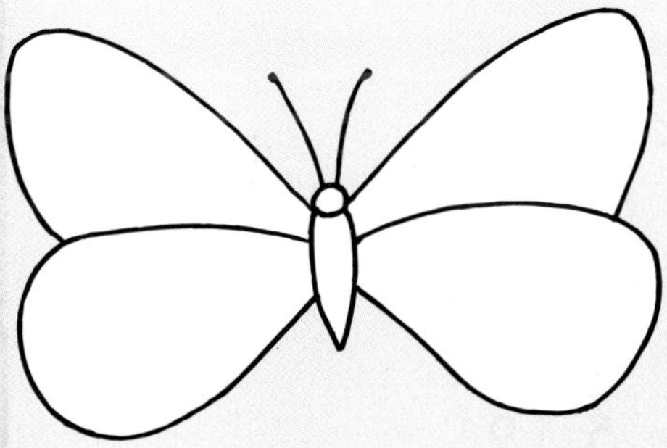

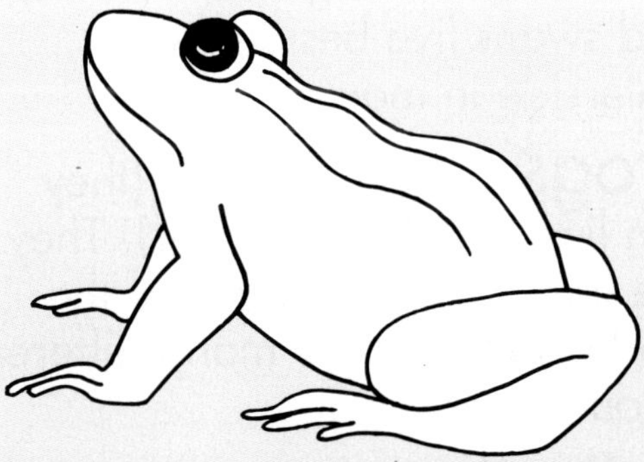

You may photocopy these pages.

Glossary

Thorax - The thorax is the largest and most important part of insects.

Bill - Bill is the mouth of a bird. Beak is another name for bill.

Trunk - The trunk is very useful to elephants as it is used to gather food.

Tail - The tail is an important part of most animals. Different kinds of animals use them in different ways.

Animals in this book

Elephants are big mammals. They live in Africa and Asia.

Swans are big birds. Ducks and swans live beside the waterside in many countries.

Frogs are amphibians (they can live in or out of water). They are found in many parts of the world. They can be many different colours.

Butterflies are insects. There are many different kinds of butterflies. They live in most parts of the world.

A B C D E F G H I J K L M N O P Q R S T U V W X Y Z

Index